Dedication

*This program is dedicated to our past and present
public protectors who have helped secure and preserve our
constitutional rights enabling us to lead safe and fulfilling lives.*

BULLY: *Being Unfriendly Lessens Liking You*
Copyright © 2018 by Bruce Brummond

ISBN 978-0-978-8486-3-7
Library of Congress Control Number: 2018935507

Illustrations by: Philip Martineau and Nolan Harris
Cover and Interior Layout by: Fusion Creative Works

www.CharacterConstructionCompany.com

Skipper says... don't be a

BULLY

because

Being Unfriendly Lessens Liking You

Written by Bruce Brummond

(Name) _____ (Date) _____
                    (Participant)   (Start Date)

This book is designed to accompany the online narrated course:

"BULLY – Being Unfriendly Lessens Liking You" by Bruce Brummond.

The online narrated course is available at: www.LearningCharacter.com

Anti-Bullying Program Introduction

This sequential experience creates a positive school culture by providing K-12 students, parents, staff and community members with easy to remember tools and techniques to effectively minimize bullying.

GOALS AND OBJECTIVES

This anti-bullying program will help you…

Analyze if you or people you know, of any age, display bullying behavior.

Learn to recognize bullying and the appropriate actions to take if you are bullied.

Learn what to do if you witness someone being victimized by a bully.

Understand your desire to develop friends and how to be a valued friend.

Learn that you can develop and maintain friendships by regularly displaying empathy.

Understand that empathy means to display your regular acts of kindness.

Acquire a set of positive self-talk tools to enhance your personal interactions.

Discover how to avoid arguments by diffusing emotionally charged situations.

Find out how to control your anger that might develop into an excuse for retaliation.

Learn to be responsible for your own actions by carefully analyzing your behavior.

Recognize if your actions will eventually help or hurt you or others.

Learn the dangers of behaviors that might develop into harmful habits.

Make sure your positive attitude helps you develop self-respect and respect for others.

Preface

Anti-social behavior creates a myriad of undesirable outcomes that can erupt into bullying. Successful student self-discipline minimizes conflicts and maximizes learning. We believe in the concepts explained in this quote for effectively educating children.

"You can't teach children to behave better by making them feel worse.

When children feel better, they behave better." — Pam Leo

We profess that everyone in school desires to have feelings of belonging, being needed and being loved. Young people can feel they belong if they are respected for being good citizens of the school community. They develop feelings of being needed if they attain knowledge and skills while learning to share those abilities with others. By practicing effective social interactions students develop feelings of belonging that enhance their feeling of self-worth. When people realize their personal value they are more likely to continue developing love for themselves and members of their community. A positive self-image greatly enhances students' learning which ultimately can create happy and fulfilling lives.

Our approach to effective education is teaching and modeling to children "what to do" rather than concentrating on "what not to do." Most children enter school eager to learn the steps to success. They are nurtured on their journey when they are provided with tools for appropriate social interaction and exercises for academic achievement.

Schools can be more effective if all students learn to "B Triple A." Bullying can be greatly minimized if students concentrate on "BAAA…Be Ambitious And Accountable." This will result in more time spent in effective learning and less time dealing with student conflicts.

We recognize that inappropriate actions can lead to punishment. We believe that applying the concepts championed in this experience will minimize discipline issues which can result in isolation and rejection culminating in lost educational opportunities.

Students exhibiting bullying behavior can create a culture of fear and disrespect throughout the entire school community, culminating in diminished student achievement.

PROGRAM OUTCOMES

Students will share their empathy with family, friends and the community.

Adults and students will procure tools to comprehend and reduce bullying behavior.

Successful interpersonal relationships produce a safe, cooperative learning environment.

A positive school culture creates higher attendance rates and increased academic achievement.

BULLY COURSE IMPLEMENTATION

1. The BULLY course provides easy to remember tools and techniques to minimize bullying by promoting positive communication throughout the entire community. The course is available in print with two year online subscriptions for computers and mobile devices.

2. Students in grades K-12, employees, parents and community members all benefit by experiencing BULLY individually and/or in groups. Younger students will need additional assistance to comprehend and implement the materials.

3. We encourage families, friends and community members to have their own BULLY Books to allow them to be engaged in the methodology the students are experiencing. Youngsters can enhance their understanding of the methodology by teaming with adults as the adults work through the exercises in their books.

4. Yes…adults can be CHAMPIONS, as well as CHAMPS on their way to becoming members of the FRIEND CLUB! Please read on to find out how this works.

5. It takes a minimum of three hours to preview the entire course. Participants can extend the experience by spending five to ten minutes per week for thirty-six weeks. We suggest covering one lesson per week. The timeline in the back of the book can be used to establish a "Word or Quote of the Week" that can be memorized and shared with the entire community.

6. The selected words and quotes can be shared with everyone: students, employees, parents, and community members. We suggest designating a person to be the organization's COACH – Channeling Our Actions Creates Happiness, to oversee implementing the methodology.

7. Most weeks have one lesson, some weeks have multiple lessons to select as the word or quote of the week. The COACH ideally will designate the word or quote of the week. The COACH will also verify that participants, called CHAMPS – Combining Hearts And Minds Propels Success, have completed the activities to qualify for a "FRIEND CLUB" Certificate.

8. We suggest that the COACH download the "FRIEND CLUB" Certificate from www.LearningCharacter.com, produce required copies, sign and distribute them to successful CHAMPS. The COACH can also maintain a published listing of the official members of the "FRIEND CLUB!"

9. If CHAMPS are using only books, teachers may elect to develop customized CHAMP examinations. A final test is available online at the conclusion of the online course.

10. While taking the course, we suggest compiling entries on the "Promise Pages." Students, referred to as CHAMPS – Connecting Hearts And Minds Propels Success, are encouraged to engage family members and community members as CHAMPIONS – Citizens Help Activate My Promises In Our Neighborhood, to assist in fulfilling their promises.

11. At the conclusion of the course the CHAMPS are asked to verify their success in fulfilling their promises by signing and dating the promise page. The CHAMPIONS are asked to also sign and date the promise page indicating the CHAMPS have completed the exercises in the book and are fulfilling their promises.

12. The BULLY course can be viewed online and/or accessed in the BULLY book. Teachers/facilitators can display the narrated online portion and lead group discussions as CHAMPS complete the corresponding exercises in their BULLY Books.

13. Individuals can complete the entire course online and/or record their answers in their BULLY Books. CHAMPS participating in the online course will automatically qualify to receive a certificate of successful course completion by receiving an eighty percent score on the final online test. A certificate of successful completion can also be downloaded from our website.

14. The book is nearly an exact copy of the online course. Most of the photos from the online course are enclosed and all of the written activities are included. We apologize for the low resolution of some of the historical photos. The images of real people, in real places, doing real things have been carefully selected to help exemplify the personalized messages. The online portion is narrated and has additional levels of responses, plus a final test and a "Friend Club" certificate.

15. The Certificate signifies the CHAMP is an official member of the "FRIEND CLUB." Hopefully the "FRIEND CLUB" members will help one another so they won't "Flub Up!" Combining the words "FRIEND" and "CLUB" can produce the word…"FLUB!"

16. All of the BULLY course activities can be embellished with essays, small group discussions, art work and role playing to practice applying non-confrontational communication skills.

17. The puzzles in the BULLY Book can be completed at any time.

18. What should CHAMPS do after they complete this course? They can be engaged in the same BULLY course the next year and/or experience our other sixteen online character building courses.

19. Questions, comments, critiques? Please contact us at www.LearningCharacter.com

```
              COACH


CHAMPIONS   CHAMPS   FRIENDS


          FRIEND CLUB
```

1. COACH*...coordinates the BULLY Course to create FRIEND CLUB Members.

2. CHAMPIONS*...help CHAMPS qualify to be members of the FRIEND CLUB.

3. CHAMPS*...people taking the course to qualify to be members of the FRIEND CLUB.
    A person can be a CHAMP and a CHAMPION at the same time.

4. FRIENDS...everyone in the community helping CHAMPS practice their promises.
    Community members can also become CHAMPS and qualify for the FRIEND CLUB.

5. FRIEND CLUB*...CHAMPS who have successfully completed the BULLY Course.

*COACH – Channeling Our Actions Creates Happiness
*CHAMPIONS – Citizens Help Activate My Promises In Our Neighborhood
*CHAMPS – Connecting Hearts And Minds Propels Success
*FRIEND CLUB - Fabulous Relationships Inspire Empathy Not Drama…
             Change Lives Undo Bullying

BULLY

Being Unfriendly Lessens Liking You

Should you ever be called a bully?

Do you enjoy making others feel bad?

Do you know what to do if you are bullied?

Are you happy with your feelings of self-worth?

Do you bully others because you are unhappy with yourself?

Have you been bullied by anyone who may need help in finding friends?

Do you use your power to hurt others or to help the world be a happier place?

Please write the words in the correct order to define BULLY.

Unfriendly   _____

You   _____

Being   _____

Lessens   _____

Liking   _____

You might be called a bully if you…push, pull, hit, fight, threaten, call people names, tease, gossip, cyber bully, and/or spread rumors. You fit the definition of a bully if you are "a person who uses strength or power to harm or intimidate those who are weaker." Should you avoid actions that might harm or intimidate others? Certainly! You should always avoid harming or intimidating others; unless you would like to suffer the consequences of your actions!

Place an "X" by the six statements that can best end this sentence.

I might be called a bully if I _____

_____ pick on someone because they are different than me.

_____ attack someone by insulting them in person or online.

_____ display my power by making someone feel bad.

_____ tease someone about something they cannot easily change.

_____ try to help people with whatever they might need.

_____ push, pull, hit someone, or use words as weapons.

_____ strike up a conversation with someone who might be alone.

_____ am always nice to everyone I know.

_____ always display empathy towards everyone I know.

_____ threaten people and call them insulting names in person or online.

Please write in the number that best describes how you feel about friends.

1 = Never   2 = Sometimes   3 = Usually   4 = Mostly   5 = Always

_____ I like having friends; having friends makes me happy.

_____ I really like most of my friends.

_____ All of my friends are nice to me.

_____ I am nice to all of my friends.

_____ I enjoy developing more friends who are nice to me.

_____ Many people I know consider me to be their friend.

_____ Sometimes I need to be nicer to some of my friends.

_____ Sometimes my friends should be nicer to me.

_____ I would like to learn how to develop more friends.

_____ I would like to learn how friends can be nicer to one another.

Please place an "X" by only one definition of a bully to end the following sentence.

A bully is a person who uses _____

_____ strength or power to help others discover happiness.

_____ their smile and kind words to help people who are lonely.

_____ strength or power to harm or intimidate those who are weaker.

_____ kindness and compassion to develop long lasting friends.

_____ their time, gifts and talents to help the world be a happier place.

How do people intimidate or harm others? By how they BEHAVE - Bullies Eliminate Happiness And Victimize Everyone. Bullies are happy to dash other people's happiness. It gives them a feeling of power over others. Bullies are fed by having control over people's emotions. They accomplish this by turning people into victims. If you feel you are being victimized by someone, tell them to stop. If they don't stop, "Walk Away Today!" Bullies need to pay close attention to how they BEHAVE.

Please write the words in the correct order to define BEHAVE.

Happiness   _____

And   _____

Bullies   _____

Victimize   _____

Eliminate   _____

Everyone   _____

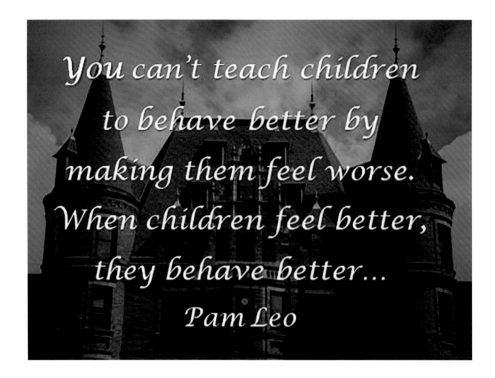

There are a myriad of undesirable outcomes of anti-social behavior that erupt into bullying. Successful student self-discipline minimizes conflicts and maximizes learning. Hopefully you agree with this quote that applies to people of all ages.

"You can't teach children to behave better by making them feel worse. When children feel better, they behave better..."
–Pam Leo

Please place the quote in the correct order by writing numbers 1, 2, 3, 4, 5 in the spaces.

_____ *to behave better by*

_____ *You can't teach children*

_____ *When children feel better,*

_____ *making them feel worse.*

_____ *they behave better...*

FRIEND
Fabulous Relationships Inspire
Empathy Not Drama

Most people feel their most valuable possession is a close FRIEND – Fabulous Relationships Inspire Empathy Not Drama. For several years while facilitating our courses people perpetually asked, how does a person develop friends? I always explained that people will want to be our friend if they enjoy being in our company. We have a much better chance of someone being our friend if we display a sincere interest in them and if we compliment them. Would you like your friends to talk about themselves all of the time and insult you? Do you ask your friends about themselves? Do you attempt to understand your friends from their perspective? Do you share empathy with your friends or spread drama?

Most people feel their most precious possession is a close FRIEND – Fabulous Relationships Inspire Empathy Not Drama!

Please write the words in the correct order to define FRIEND.

Inspire   Fabulous   Not   Relationships   Empathy   Drama

_____   _____   _____   _____   _____   _____

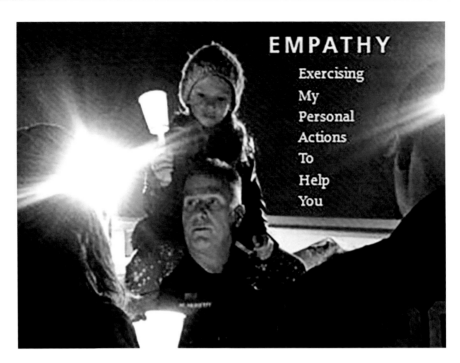

EMPATHY – Exercising My Personal Actions To Help You. Do you shine the light of hope and goodness on your friends, especially in times of darkness? Do you allow others to lift you up? Do you lift others up? Do you search for ways to help others in their times of need or do you simply talk about helping others? Can you relate when you have helped others in their times of need? Do you have memories of how others have helped you in your times of need?

Place an "X" by the five statements that best define EMPATHY.

_____ If I see someone being bullied I will tell the bully to stop.

_____ Spreading DRAMA – Debilitating Rumors Activate Malicious Attitudes.

_____ Helping someone, even if they have not asked for my help.

_____ I will tell an adult if I tell a bully to stop and they continue bullying people.

_____ Knowing what should be done to help someone who has been hurt.

_____ Helping someone seek help if they have been bullied.

_____ Wishing that none of my friends will ever be the victim of a bully.

_____ Feeling sorry for someone and thinking that someday I will help them.

_____ If I witness bullying: see something, say something, save someone!

Please place an "X" by seven ways you like to display EMPATHY.

_____ I enjoy sharing my gifts, talents and time to help others.

_____ I enjoy showing others why I am superior to them to inflate my ego.

_____ I will talk with someone who might be alone to help them feel included.

_____ I enjoy displaying my power over others to make me feel important.

_____ I enjoy helping others understand and resolve their personal problems.

_____ I get a thrill out of harshly criticizing others to bolster my ego.

_____ I display RESPECT – Recognizing Everyone's Strengths Produces Exceptional Caring Teams.

_____ I enjoy lifting others up in their times of darkness by listening to their struggles.

_____ I ask people how I can help them and follow up with their suggestions.

_____ I really enjoy helping people discover success to help them be happy.

Let's always give a "Thumbs Up" to our first responders when we see them in uniform. Our first responders' mission is to help us lead safe lives. Hopefully you will always remember to thank them for sharing their empathy!

Please fill in the blanks with the underlined words to end the following sentence. It would be appropriate if we give a "Thumbs Up" or a "Thumbs Down" to:

<u>Police Officers</u>   <u>Fire Fighters</u>   <u>Bullies</u>   <u>Military Personnel</u>

_____ for protecting us from fires.

_____ for protecting our country.

_____ for hurting people.

_____ for protecting us from harm.

**BAAA
Be Ambitious And Accountable**

Can you always Be a Triple A Person? Can you always Be Ambitious And Accountable? Can you travel down your road of life while being responsible for your own actions? Can you avoid a life of turbulence by understanding when your path might lead to problems and you need to stop what you are doing? Do you demonstrate that you are ambitious and accountable? Do you place blame and bully others because of your lack of accepting responsibility for your own behavior? Will you have a better chance of experiencing a happy and fulfilling life if you will always "B Triple A?"

Please write in the number to indicate how often you are a "B Triple A Person."

1 = Never   2 = Sometimes   3 = Usually   4 = Mostly   5 = Always

_____ I am a self-starter and very motivated.

_____ I show up on time, listen carefully and work hard.

_____ I thoroughly prepare for my responsibilities.

_____ I avoid blaming others if I do not reach my goals.

_____ I avoid making excuses if I do not reach my goals.

_____ I honestly state the facts to help others understand.

_____ If at all possible I help others attain success.

_____ I avoid acting like a bully; I am nice to people.

_____ I am an enviable role model; I lead by example.

TRY means To Respect Yourself. If you don't like the outcome try again, try harder next time, or try a little different direction. While serving as a school district administrator I surprised a staff member with a set of handbells for his "special needs students." He was dumbfounded! While stammering in disbelief he blurted out that he thought I was stupid to even suggest he try such an outlandish project. He explained that he knew absolutely nothing about handbells. He certainly wasn't reassured when I added "there are now two of us in this office who know absolutely nothing about handbells." I assured our empathetic educator that I had faith in his ability to learn about the instruments and that he would develop his students into an incredible musical organization. I said "Harry…let's give it a TRY!"

During the next school year the "special needs students" staged fifty-two performances. Two things always happened: they put the audience in tears and received standing ovations because we…gave it…a TRY! Were we afraid? Certainly! Fear can motivate us to try harder. Always remember the four magic words that can lead to success: give it a TRY and TRY means To Respect Yourself!

Place an "X" by the six responses
you would appreciate others to share.

If I try something and fail to reach my goal I would appreciate if people would say.

_____ Let me help you reach your goal; I respect you so much for trying!

_____ Congratulations for giving it a TRY; it means To Respect Yourself.

_____ Try again, try harder next time, maybe redirect your efforts.

_____ You worked hard for a long time; congratulations on your persistence!

_____ You should have known you weren't smart enough to succeed.

_____ You were stupid to try because you failed…ha…ha…ha!

_____ I knew you were going to fail; you always mess up and fail.

_____ You are a great role model; you inspire people to never give up!

_____ Your selflessness inspires everyone who knows you to keep trying.

_____ That will lead you to success and make me look lazy. Don't try so hard!

Place an "X" by the six best statements that will encourage people to TRY.

In the future when others TRY but fail to reach their goal I will plan on saying.

_____ Congratulations on your START – Success Takes A Realistic Try.

_____ You were stupid to try because you failed…ha…ha…ha!

_____ That will lead you to success and make me look lazy. Don't try so hard!

_____ You worked hard for a long time; congratulations on your persistence!

_____ You should have known that you weren't smart enough to succeed.

_____ You are a great role model; you inspire people to never give up!

_____ Your selflessness inspires everyone who knows you to keep trying.

_____ I knew you were going to fail; you always mess up and fail.

_____ Try again, try harder next time, maybe redirect your efforts.

_____ Let me help you reach your goal; I respect you so much for trying!

"If you can't say anything nice about somebody, don't say anything at all!"

The Mothers of the world perpetually remind us…"If you can't say anything nice about somebody, don't say anything at all!" Would our world be a much happier place if everyone abided by our Mothers' kind words? Is it possible for you to always consider what your Mother would want you to say before you say it?

Place one "X" to properly end the following sentence.

The Mothers of the world remind us _____

_____ to bully everyone possible to display that we are very important and powerful.

_____ if you can't say anything nice about somebody, don't say anything at all.

_____ to criticize others for trying so you won't feel bad if they become successful.

_____ to always place blame on others so you won't feel guilty about not trying.

SMILE - Sure Makes It Lots Easier. Do you think this young Cub Scout is proudly displaying that he belongs to an organization; his membership is validated because he is needed and the icing on the cake is that he is loved? There are many groups for us to join that provide us with positive feelings of sharing goodness. Do you belong to organizations that bring a smile to your face?

This is very real; I just told Skipper that his Dad and Mom will soon be leaving to attend an event of one of our community organizations. Can you inquire about groups you might join? Humans flourish with meaningful social interactions. Research has shown that social isolation can compound mental health issues. For your emotional wellness please attempt to be involved with organizations that help you smile!

A sensational way to be liked by more people and develop more friends is to SMILE.

Please write the words in the correct order to define the word SMILE.

Makes   _____

It   _____

Easier   _____

Sure   _____

Lots   _____

"If you want to find a friend, be a friend!"

Friend

Many people wonder how to find a FRIEND. Always remember…"If you want to find a friend be a friend!" You can find friends by simply seeking out someone who might be alone. We have all experienced feeling alone and we have greatly appreciated a warm welcome from someone. We can always welcome others…wherever it might be!

All friends have one thing in common: there was a first time they met. Provide yourself opportunities to develop friends by introducing yourself to others. Get to know people by asking them questions about where they are from, their interests, their families, their future goals and then follow those questions up with discussions.

Questions like these can lead to developing valuable new friendships that may last for a lifetime!

Place an "X" in one space to correctly end the following sentence.

Many people will be your friend and help you celebrate _____

_____ if you are nice to people, you will have many friends.

_____ if you are a bully and people are afraid of you.

As I mentioned, everyone desires to have a feeling of belonging, that belonging is validated if we are needed and the icing on the cake is if we are loved. My Brother, who was two years older than me, experienced all three of these ingredients of a happy life. Our family and friends loved helping him celebrate his fourth birthday. He experienced a very successful life because he belonged, he was needed and he was loved.

After being the best of friends for nearly three quarters of a century do you think I miss him? Does the hole in my heart indicate the depth of my feelings of belonging with him, of needing him and of loving him? Our most valuable possessions are our close friends. Be kind to your friends, appreciate them, cherish them, share empathy with them. Hopefully when your friend leaves for the final time you will remember sharing the joys of belonging, being needed and being loved.

This is the last time I saw my brother aboard his commercial salmon boat at Neah Bay, Washington. Would all of our relationships be better if we treated every interaction as though it would be the last time we would see that person?

Place an "X" by four statements to best end the following sentence.

I have feelings of belonging, being needed and being loved when I _____

_____ tell people that I belong to a team, club, family or group.

_____ share evil so people will notice me for being extremely different.

_____ follow expectations of belonging to a team, club, family or group.

_____ display my power by bullying others to make them feel bad.

_____ share goodness; I will have a good chance of being loved.

_____ make everybody mad at me because I want to be noticed.

_____ draw attention to myself, even though people don't like my actions.

_____ try to fit in by bullying others until people laugh with me.

_____ treat everyone like it will be the last time I will see that person.

Let's discover your strengths and build on them…I am a…teacher! Are you a teacher? Certainly! Everyone is a teacher! Who is your primary student? Yourself! Possibly the most important thing we can learn is learning how to learn. In other words: how to teach ourselves! Our Empowerment Course teaches the "Five C's of Teaching." The Five C's are: Connect, Challenge, Channel, Check and that builds Confidence. Remember the Five C's anytime you teach anybody anything, especially yourself…we are all teachers!

Place an "X" by one statement to end the following sentence.

The teacher who is responsible for teaching me the most _____

_____ is available in an online course.

_____ is the person who taught my favorite class.

_____ is the person currently wearing my clothing.

_____ is the person who was paid the most to teach me.

_____ is the person with the most advanced college degree.

_____ is the person who is the most intelligent.

If you are rejected by someone you may have bullied it might be time to say you are SORRY – Success Often Requires Rescinding Yourself. Is there a good chance your friends reject you if you bully them? A sincere apology can be the first step in rebuilding the bridges you may have burned. How do you remain friends with many people? Repair relationships by learning to begin an appropriate apology with a sincere sorry!

If we offend someone it is always best to say we are SORRY.

Please write the words in the correct order to define SORRY.

Yourself _____

Requires _____

Rescinding _____

Success _____

Often _____

Apology Plan

Write an apology for something offensive you may have done or not done.

1. I am sorry and I apologize because I now understand that I offended you when I said (or did)…

    _____

    _____

    _____

2. I said (or did) it because I was…

    _____

    _____

    _____.

3. I was wrong and I should have said (or done)…

    _____

    _____

    _____.

4. In the future I am planning to…

    _____

    _____

    _____ so that doesn't happen again.

5. I sincerely hope you accept my apology because I value our relationship more than…

    _____

    _____

    _____!

Many people make copies of this form available for anyone who would like to make an apology.
You might consider keeping a supply at hand. All relationships need occasional rebooting.
A sincere apology is like a trip to the hospital emergency room to patch up friendships.

All of us need to sometimes stop and think about what we are saying or doing because we might be acting like a bully. This can be the meaning of STOP - Some Things Offend People.

We need to avoid criticizing others about their appearance, clothes, family and friends. We should never pick on someone about something that may be difficult or impossible to change like skin color, body size, heredity, or past actions.

Spreading rumors or gossip in person or online can create a tornado of torment. Never criticize others when they fail to reach their goals; simply encourage them to keep trying. Here's a tough one…always avoid criticizing others when they are more successful than you. Offer them a sincere congratulation and appreciate them as a precious role model!

Place an "X" by six statements to best end the following sentence.

People should always STOP before they say:

_____ I'm happy to see you; I really appreciate being your friend.

_____ my clothes are nicer than yours; other clothes would never help you!

_____ can I help you understand how to complete that assignment?

_____ congratulations on your progress; you are really blossoming.

_____ the color of my skin proves that I am a lot better than you.

_____ people don't like you because of where you live.

_____ you certainly aren't very cute and you aren't popular; look at me!

_____ your name makes you sound stupid and you live up to your name!

_____ I'll spread rumors and tell people online that I am better than you!

_____ I practice the ROSE principle…Respect Others; Share Empathy!

I always STOP before I say anything hurtful.

Place an "X" by the four statements to best end the following sentence.

I spread empathy by saying:

_____ I'm happy to see you; I really appreciate being your friend.

_____ my clothes are nicer than yours; other clothes would never help you!

_____ can I help you understand how to complete that assignment?

_____ congratulations on your progress; you are really blossoming.

_____ the color of my skin proves that I am much better than you.

_____ people don't like you because of where you live.

_____ you certainly aren't very cute and you aren't popular; look at me!

_____ your name makes you sound stupid and you live up to your name!

_____ I'll spread rumors and tell people online that I am better than you!

_____ I practice the ROSE principle…Respect Others; Share Empathy!

What should you do if you are bullied?

What should you do if you are bullied?

1. If you are bullied…tell the bully to stop!

2. If they don't stop…"Walk Away Today!"

3. If they continue to bully…tell an adult.

4. If you are not satisfied with the adult's response…seek help from a different adult.

If you are bullied make certain to take notes of the details, so you have an accurate accounting of the situation to share with adults.

Please complete these four statements by writing in the underlined suggestions.

<u>tell the bully to stop!</u>   <u>"Walk Away Today!"</u>   <u>tell an adult.</u>   <u>seek help from a different adult.</u>

If you are bullied, _____

If they don't stop, _____

If they continue to bully, _____

If the adult fails to stop the bully, _____

Never Insult Compliment Everyone

This is a group of second graders in 1950 at East Port Orchard Elementary School performing a "Maypole Dance." The teacher asked "will one of you boys be really NICE and join the girls in the "Maypole Dance?" Guess who joined the girls? A second grader decided a boy is never too young to be NICE - Never Insult Compliment Everyone. Can you go beyond your level of comfort to be nice to others, even if you aren't doing a "Maypole Dance?"

We will have more friends if we are always NICE.

Please write the words in the correct order to define NICE.

Compliment   _____

Never   _____

Everyone   _____

Insult   _____

Issuing Negative Statements Usually Leaves Turmoil. Do people who INSULT you create turmoil? Because of your fear of more insults do you attempt to avoid that person in the future? Does a person making insults feel victorious when insults stir up the emotions of the victim? If we overreact to insults will more insults likely come our way?

Insults propel turmoil, harassment, bullying, arguing, fighting and violence. Would the world be a much happier place if we compliment people rather than spread insults? Remember to always be NICE - Never Insult Compliment Everyone!

Please place a number 1-5 in each space to help determine if you spread INSULTS.

1 = Never   2 = Sometimes   3 = Usually   4 = Mostly   5 = Always

_____ I like to say mean things to people so they get mad at me.

_____ I compliment people and avoid insulting them with peer pressure.

_____ If I hear someone bullying anybody I tell them to stop.

_____ I like helping bullies pick on other people because it is fun.

_____ I have lost friends because of what I have said about them.

_____ People like me because I am always really nice to them.

_____ I feel that "peer pressure is only ear pressure, not fear pressure."

_____ I tell people the truth even if it really hurts their feelings.

_____ I think that sometimes I act like a bully.

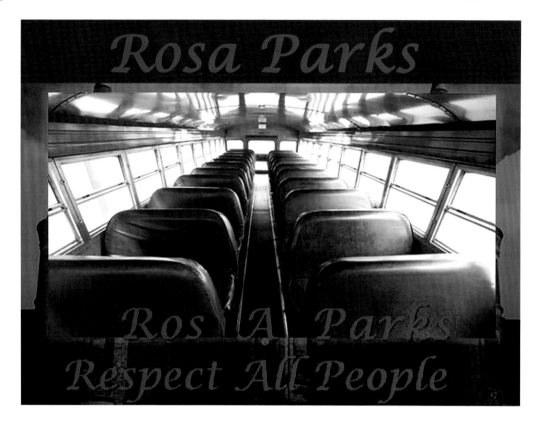

The person who has been called the mother of the civil rights movement was a bus passenger in Montgomery, Alabama. Rosa Parks, an African-American seamstress, stepped onto a bus on December 1, 1955 and refused to proceed to the back where she was instructed to ride.

She defiantly sat in the front seat of the public bus. Her refusal to abide by the rules regarding segregation started a fire storm of protests that brought attention to racial discrimination in the United States. She provided Martin Luther King with the impetus to carry forth with the civil rights movement. What would our world be like if everyone honored her legacy by enacting this concept? Ros…A…Parks stands for "Respect All People!"

Please place an "X" in the proper space to correctly end the following statement.

Rosa Parks reminds us to…

_____ "Respect All People!"

_____ "Rudely Attack People!"

STADIUM HIGH SCHOOL CHOIR
NORMANDY LIBERATION AND BICENTENNIAL MUSIC CELEBRATION

What does the word ASK mean to you? Let's explore a concept you can employ to make a positive change in your communications with others. It boils down to how we ask to seek change. What if ASK means Always Seek Knowledge? Do you always kindly answer questions that others ask of you? Would you like others to Always Speak Kindly when you ASK?

We change by learning new information. We freely ask questions if we are not belittled by the reply. Do you wish that your questions would always result in a kind response? Do you always respond to questions in a kind manner?

We should always nicely respond to questions that others ASK.

Please write the words in the proper order of asking and answering.

Always _____

Seek _____

Kindly _____

Knowledge _____

Always _____

Speak _____

TEACH - Try Engaging All Children Happily. We are all teachers; ideally we enjoy sharing our knowledge with others. I have designated the Five C's of teaching that describe almost everything we do, including the steps in learning. This Dad is instructing his Son to the intricacies of carpentry. This Father is activating the Five C's of effective teaching: Connect, Challenge, Channel, Check and that builds Confidence. Can you describe how the Five C's of teaching are being practiced in this photo? Let me explain.

Do you think Dave asked his Son if he would like to build this project? Do you see how important it is to ask in a kind manner so the connection and the challenge take place?

Is the gentleman channeling the process by holding onto the parts so his Son can strike the nail? Do you think they carefully checked the project to see if they assembled it properly?

Do you think the boy now has confidence that he can learn to build things?

Locate and place the Five C's in the correct order by numbering them 1, 2, 3, 4, 5.

_____ Connect   _____ Creativity   _____ Challenge   _____ Channel

_____ Captivate   _____ Confusion   _____ Check   _____ Correct

_____ Confidence   _____ Confrontation

All human beings get mad…anger give us an adrenaline rush to help us survive. We need to be very cautious when we get MAD because Meanness Always Destroys. If you realize you are getting MAD immediately breathe through your nose. Can you say anything if you are breathing through your nose?

If you are standing, if at all possible place your hands in your pockets and sit down. Will this help you avoid overreacting, while being mad, that might create more problems in the emotionally charged situation?

Place numbers 1-6 in order of what to do if you get MAD – Meanness Always Destroys.

_____ If you get MAD – Meanness Always Destroys…

_____ After trying this…it still

_____ breathe through your nose and

_____ put your hands in your pockets.

_____ might be best to "Walk Away Today!"

_____ If you are standing: sit down.

Is it the problem or how we react to the problem that causes the most problems? If we immediately fight back against the problem created by a bully, the problem will probably escalate; sadly it will probably just get worse.

People act like bullies because they desire to have power over others. If at all possible, what if you react by "feeding" the bully with kindness? Do you think the bully might actually simply be searching for friends?

Fill each blank with one word.

Here is a clue, you will notice a pattern!

Is it the _____

or how we react to the _____

that causes the most _____?

Everyone wants to feel important, valued,
needed, and appreciated to hopefully attain
respect. Bullies mistakenly fulfill these goals in
unacceptable ways by how they display their

POWER

Perpetually Offending Will Erode Respect

Purposely Offending With Every Response

Pushing Over Welldoers Eliminates Respect

People's Offensive Words Eliminate Respect

People's Offensive Words Exemplify Rudeness

Everyone wants to feel important, valued, needed and appreciated to hopefully attain respect. Bullies mistakenly fulfill these goals in unacceptable ways by how they display their POWER – Perpetually Offending Will Erode Respect…Purposely Offending With Every Response…Pushing Over Welldoers Eliminates Respect…People's Offensive Words Eliminate Respect…People's Offensive Words Exemplify Rudeness.

Hopefully you display your power in a respectful manner.

Christopher Reeve acted in movies as Superman. Do you agree with his quote regarding POWER? "What makes Superman a hero is not that he has POWER, but that he has the wisdom and the maturity to use the POWER wisely."

Please place an "X" by the correct answer.

_____ Yes, we should always use our POWER to help people, not to hurt people!

_____ No, the best way to display our POWER is to hurt people by behaving like a bully!

Feeling important, valued, needed, and
appreciated provides us with feelings of respect.
We can receive feelings of respect by how we share our

POWER

Plan On Winning Everyone's Respect
Proving Our Worth Establishes Respect
Personal Optimism Will Encourage Respect
Pleasing Others With Everlasting Recognition
Perpetually Offering Wisdom Elevates Respect

Feeling important, valued, needed, and appreciated provides us with feelings of respect. We can receive feelings of respect by how we share our POWER – Plan On Winning Everyone's Respect...Proving Our Worth Establishes Respect...Personal Optimism Will Encourage Respect...Pleasing Others With Everlasting Recognition...Perpetually Offering Wisdom Elevates Respect. Hopefully you share your power in these ways!

Please place an "X" by five positive ways to display your POWER.

_____ Plan On Winning Everyone's Respect

_____ Perpetually Offending Will Erode Respect

_____ Proving Our Worth Establishes Respect

_____ Pushing Over Welldoers Eliminates Respect

_____ Personal Optimism Will Encourage Respect

_____ Pleasing Others With Everlasting Recognition

_____ People's Offensive Words Eliminate Respect

_____ Perpetually Offering Wisdom Elevates Respect

ROLE MODEL – Reflecting Our Leader's Example Makes Our Deeds Endure Lifelong. Should you carefully select your role models? Certainly! Hopefully you have the opportunity to select leaders you would like to use as examples. If not search for some new examples!

Do you think this toddler is learning to fulfill challenges? Do you think he is learning that success takes a lot of hard work? Do you imagine that his father introduced him to digging clams in a positive, fun manner? Do you think the boy was learning to Control All Negativism; Develop Optimism? Sure he was developing a CANDO attitude!

Do you think the boy was upset when they reached the daily clam limit and had to stop searching for success?

Here's a clue to the answer of all these questions. Do you think the ocean is wet?

Please place an "X" by what you can learn from your ROLE MODEL.

_____ I can learn to be a bully by watching how people bully me.

_____ I can learn to fulfill challenges by working hard to achieve success.

_____ I can learn that peer pressure is only ear pressure, not fear pressure.

_____ I CANDO - Control All Negativism Develop Optimism.

_____ I can learn that water is wet.

_____ I can learn to love turning problems into challenges.

_____ I can learn to be mean to others.

_____ I can learn that there are many fun things to do in life.

_____ I can learn that it is very, very important to always be kind.

_____ I can learn to be careful how I act because I am a role model.

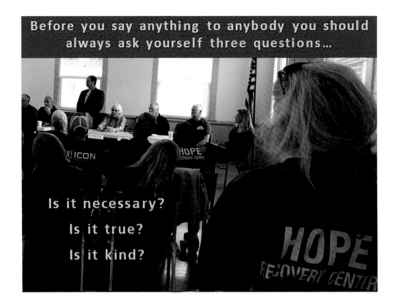

Before you say anything to anybody you should always ask yourself three questions.

Is it necessary? Is it true? Is it kind? This was a public forum presented by board members of the "Hope Recover Center", a non-profit organization located near Tacoma, Washington. The group is proceeding with plans to build a large residential addiction treatment center.

The board members explained to the community why the treatment center is necessary. They also shared true stories of the life and death consequences of addictions. The entire presentation displayed their desire to share their kindness with people struggling with the disease of addiction. Always remember to give your responses the three way test…is it necessary, is it true, is it kind?

Please place an "X" by three things you should consider before you say anything to anybody.

_____ Is it necessary?

_____ Is it funny?

_____ Will it make me more popular?

_____ Is it effectively placing blame?

_____ Does it make me look better?

_____ Is it kind?

_____ Will I get everybody's attention?

_____ Will it help me put others down?

_____ Is it true?

Years ago as I was floating down the Hoh River my rubber raft became entangled in a log jam and I was flung into the raging river! As I was tumbling along the river bottom I thought "will it help or hurt if I drown?" Decades later that statement rings more true than ever.

As we select what we say to others, what if we perpetually ask ourselves: "will it 'Help Or Hurt' me, will it 'Help Or Hurt' others?" The "HOH Principle" can guide us in making all of our decisions. Will it "Help or Hurt" me? Will it "Help Or Hurt" others?

Please place an "X" by six things the HOH Principle will help you decide.

The HOH Principle will help me decide:

_____ if what I am saying is true?

_____ if I should lie by blaming others?

_____ if I should steal from someone?

_____ if my friends like me a lot?

_____ if what I am saying is kind?

_____ if what I am saying is necessary?

_____ if I am acting like a bully?

_____ if I am better than others?

Our oldest Grandson has a brilliant idea of how to avoid being addicted to nicotine, alcohol and drugs. He explains it very simply: "Be Smart; Don't Start!" Statistics confirm that one experience with nicotine or just one encounter with an illicit drug can begin people on a path to hook them forever. Alcohol abuse can also culminate in addiction leading to an untimely death. Please remember: "Be Smart; Don't Start!" Please share these four words with everyone you know. It is a thousand times easier to not begin an addiction than trying to stop the horrific cycle of chemical dependency!

Please place an "X" by six ways to end this statement.

The best way to avoid being hooked on potential harmful habits is to always remember:

Be Smart;_____

_____ Don't Start!   _____ Don't Start!!   _____ Don't Start!!!

_____ Don't Start!!!!   _____ Don't Start!!!!!   _____ Don't Start!!!!!!

Please place a number 1-5 in each space to indicate how you feel about harmful things.

1= No   2 = I'm not sure   3 = I try not to   4 = I might   5 = Yes

_____ If someone gives me a pill, no matter what it is, I will swallow it.

_____ I will smoke anything to give me feelings of belonging to a group.

_____ I will drink out of a container without knowing what I'm drinking.

_____ I will give or sell someone my family's prescription medications.

_____ Nicotine, prescription drugs and alcohol are harmless if they're legal.

_____ If I steal from someone, it's their fault because they weren't careful.

_____ It is always safe to "self-medicate" for a long time if it is legal.

_____ My family safely discards prescription drugs that we no longer require.

_____ I know someone who died because of smoking, alcohol or drugs.

_____ I can be jailed or possibly die because of smoking, alcohol or drugs.

Please place a number 1-5 in each space to indicate how you would like to end the following sentence.

1 = I disagree   2 = I hope not   3 = Not sure   4 = I might   5 = I'm all in

To experience a happy and fulfilling life I promise to myself that I will _____

_____ never begin using nicotine products of any kind.

_____ never be involved in any way with any kind of illegal drugs.

_____ never take more prescription medication than I absolutely require.

_____ never take something, without permission, that doesn't belong to me.

_____ never consume alcohol if it has the potential of hurting me or others.

_____ remember that peer pressure is only ear pressure not fear pressure.

_____ never apply peer pressure if it has the possibility of hurting someone.

_____ share my concerns about harmful habits with caring friends and adults.

_____ admit to myself and others if I flub up and develop harmful habits.

_____ seek help if I flub up and start habits that might hurt me or others.

Does it look like Skipper likes the way the Professor ACTS? Do you think Skipper's friend will "Always Care To Share?" Do you "Always Care To Share?" Do you like to be with people who always share kindness and fun times? Do you have friends who share kindness and fun times? Remember…if we "Always Care To Share" we will have more friends!

Please complete this survey by placing an "X" by how you participate in the following ACTS – Always Care To Share!

_____ I try to always compliment others and not insult them.

_____ I enjoy sharing my time, talents and treasures with everyone possible.

_____ If someone is alone I attempt to join them and develop a new friend.

_____ If at all possible I will help someone who seems to be having a bad day.

_____ I share my time with people by listening and attempting to help them.

_____ I enjoy helping someone even if they haven't asked for my help.

_____ I enjoy displaying that I CARE by sharing "Compassion And Respect Everyday."

_____ It's up to me to be a self-starter to always share myself with others.

_____ We need to always remind ourselves that we are "all in the same boat!"

TEASE – To Enjoy A Spirited Encounter. Are there times we might say things that aren't necessary and true? Certainly! Should the things we say still be kind? Certainly! We can enjoy sharing humor, if it is kind! Sharing humor that isn't kind can be defined as bullying! Might we be somewhat untruthful while we're teasing someone? Certainly! Many times the humor is entangled in finding the truth contained in the spirited experience. Enjoy sharing humor by nicely teasing others; just make certain you always share kindness! Remember avoid hurting anyone; avoid being a bully!

Please place an "X" by three acceptable ways To Enjoy A Spirited Encounter.

_____ It's fine to tease until someone feels bad if it strengthens my ego!

_____ It's fine to tease others if it is kind, not hurtful.

_____ It's fine to tease someone if they are unsuccessful.

_____ It's fine to tease someone about what they cannot easily change.

_____ It's fine to tease to make me look better than others.

_____ It's fine to tease in a way that puts others down and lifts me up.

_____ It's fine to tease by sharing humor to lighten up tense situations.

_____ It's fine to tease someone if they are physically different than me.

_____ It's fine to tease by disguising the truth, then divulging it.

The only way to win an argument is not to argue!

Dale Carnegie said "The only way to win an argument is not to argue!" Recently Mary Ann and I discussed where to spend a day with our oldest Grandson. I suggested we visit the zoo. She disagreed…did we argue…no! As I kept my mouth shut, Oma explained why we should spend our special day visiting Mt. Rainier. She explained that it was going to be a clear day, no wind and a pleasant temperature. Does it look like we were extremely happy she suggested this adventure?

Do you think an argument took place when the four year old insisted on walking up to the top of the mountain? Did we explain all of the reasons why walking to the top wouldn't be such a good idea? Did we offer him "facts not attacks" so he could make the decision to not attempt to scale the mountain that afternoon? Did we argue? No! We stated facts to empower him to make an informed decision. Whew!

Please write out the Dale Carnegie quote in the correct order.

way to _____

The only _____

an argument _____

win _____

to argue! _____

is not _____

What should you do if you are bullied? Proceed through the steps we previously suggested then if at all possible just "Walk Away Today!" If possible, cease associating with the bully.

Hopefully you can develop friends who influence you in "sweet ways" not "sour ways!"

Does it look like these students were displaying their appreciation of the "sweet times" they were experiencing while on a performance tour with their school choir?

Remember if you aren't having a sweet time and you are being bullied "Walk Away Today!"

Please place an "X" by four things you should potentially do if you are bullied.

_____ Tell the bully to stop.

_____ Start a fight with the bully.

_____ "Walk Away Today!"

_____ Treat the bully exactly how they treated you.

_____ Tell an adult you are being bullied.

_____ Stand up to the bully and start making threats.

_____ Consider telling another adult about the bully.

_____ Start untrue rumors online about the bully.

Can we always WOW one another? What if we always do what we say we are going to do? What if we "Walk Our Words?" What would you do if a Mom you know stated, "You said you were going to walk up to the top of that building?" Would you say, "Sure, I'll do what I said I was going to do…please join me…let's "Walk Our Words!"

How should we decide how to WOW others? Turn the word "WOW" upside down and ask yourself…what would my MOM want me to do? Many people's major complaint about others is that they do not do what they say they are going to do. Let's take a look in the mirror.

Do you do what you say you're going to do? Can your word be trusted? Do you apply yourself? Are you responsible for your own actions? Are you nice to others? Are you selfish? What if we treat everyone with kindness? What if we avoid unnecessarily criticizing others and be nice? What if we treat everyone how we would like to be treated? What if we never, ever, ever display our power over others by bullying them?

Ask yourself, "what vision did my Mom have for me when I was born?" Always remember, what helps us decide how to "Walk Our Words?" Turn the word WOW upside down. What does it spell? Ask yourself, "What would she want me to do?" The world would be a much happier place if everyone fulfilled their Mom's vision.

Please write in a number to rate
each possible ending of the following sentence.

1 = Never   2 = Occasionally   3 = Sometimes   4 = Usually   5 = Always

Everyone should _____

_____ do what they say they are going to do.

_____ attack people online and spread lies about them.

_____ avoid displaying their power by bullying others.

_____ avoid harmful habits and work hard for a happy life.

_____ develop many very close lifelong friends.

_____ display empathy to everyone, especially those in need.

_____ be a role model of always displaying respect.

_____ treat others the way they would like to be treated.

_____ develop their gifts and talents to share, not steal.

_____ avoid hurting anyone while disregarding peer pressure.

Please write in a number to indicate how you are attempting to fulfill your Mom's vision.

1 = Never   2 = Occasionally   3 = Sometimes   4 = Usually   5 = Always

I am fulfilling my Mom's vision by _____

_____ doing what I say I am going to do.

_____ attacking people on line and telling lies about them.

_____ displaying my power by acting like a bully.

_____ avoiding harmful habits and experiencing a happy life.

_____ developing many lifelong friends who are positive role models.

_____ displaying empathy to everyone, especially those in need.

_____ being a role model by disrespecting myself and others.

_____ treating others the way I would like to be treated.

_____ developing my gifts and talents to share, not steal.

_____ not hurting myself or others while disregarding peer pressure.

Always Trying To Improve Takes Unswerving Dedication Everyday

ATTITUDE

Do you think these boys will catch some monster salmon? It all depends on their ATTITUDE – Always Trying To Improve Takes Unswerving Dedication Everyday! My Sons were very dedicated to improving their fishing techniques. They kept trying and trying and trying to successfully fulfill their dreams of boating huge king salmon.

Does it look like they knew that it's "OK to go slow just don't stop?" Did they pay any attention to bullies who criticized their attitude about working so hard to catch fish? Will your relationships improve if you perpetually try to improve how you treat people? Will you encourage people to be successful or criticize them for working so hard? Will you have more friends if you display a great attitude?

Always displaying a positive ATTITUDE will help you avoid negativism and fulfill your vision of success.

Please write the words in the correct order to define ATTITUDE.

To Improve   _____

Takes Unswerving   _____

Everyday!   _____

Dedication   _____

Always Trying   _____

The true test of our value is how we value ourselves.

When you reflect on how this experience is impacting your life, I hope this statement sums up your feelings, "The true test of our value is how we value ourselves." This quote took us a long time to develop…I hope it resonates with you for the rest of your life!

Please write out the "Personal Value" quote in the correct order.

is how   _____

our value   _____

The true   _____

ourselves.   _____

we value   _____

test of   _____

Throughout our lives we strive to be HAPPY - Habits And Purpose Please You. Does it look like my Brother and I were happily preparing to display our talents in our Holiday Band Concert? Do you think we were focused on bullying people or joining our friends in band to share our music with the audience? Did our school band give us feelings of belonging, being needed and being loved? Did the band members bully one another or did they help each other improve? We had great attitudes that helped us be very happy!

Please place an "X" by the ways to end the following sentence that will help make you HAPPY.

It makes me happy when I am able to _____

_____ apply my gifts and talents to help others.

_____ get mad and make people feel bad.

_____ practice unhealthy habits that hurt my body and soul.

_____ help other people discover happiness by sharing my empathy.

_____ keep trying and trying and trying to fulfill my challenges.

_____ develop and enjoy many very valuable friendships.

_____ prove that I have power over others by bullying them.

_____ encourage someone to bully others and celebrate their actions.

_____ work hard to fulfill my purpose in life by helping others.

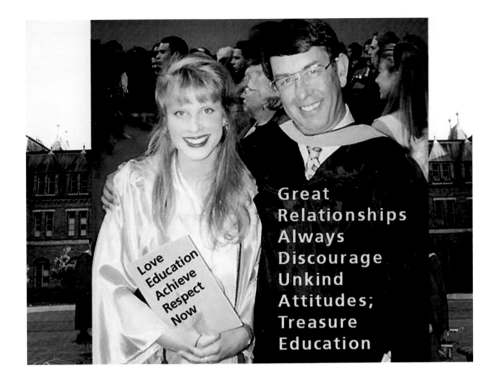

We spend our lives developing meaningful relationships to help us LEARN – Love Education; Achieve Respect Now. Anti-social behavior interferes with relationships and places our educational success in jeopardy. Success has a much better chance of coming to fruition if we learn to cooperate with others. Bullying dramatically disrupts our path to leading a happy life. If we do well in school we can celebrate our learning when we GRADUATE - Great Relationships Always Discourage Unkind Attitudes; Treasure Education!

One of the most valuable lessons learned in school is learning how to LEARN.

Please write the words in the correct order to define the word LEARN.

Respect   _____

Achieve   _____

Education   _____

Love   _____

Now   _____

FUTURE
Forget Undoing The Undoable; Refocus Efforts

Let's look to Ireland as a role model of how to forget trying to change your past and focus on improving your FUTURE - Forget Undoing the Undoable; Refocus Efforts!

In the sixth century the Skellig Michael Islands became a Monastery inhabited by a small group of Monks. The Monastery has been uninhabited for over a thousand years. The Irish people planned for the Islands' future by leaving the remnants of the Monastery unchanged. The islands look exactly as they did in the sixth century.

You may have seen their future plans show up on the big screen; several very famous movies have been filmed on these Islands. Yes, the Irish people are not trying to undo their past; they have planned for their future. I hope this example will help you forget about trying to change your past and focus on improving your future! Remember to START - Success Takes A Realistic Try!

We need to always let go of the past and focus on improving our FUTURE.

Please write the words in the correct order to define FUTURE.

Undoable;   _____

Forget   _____

Undoing   _____

The   _____

Efforts   _____

Refocus   _____

FUTURE
Forget Undoing The Undoable; Refocus Efforts

Please write in a number to rate the ending of each sentence.

1 = Never   2 = Occasionally   3 = Sometimes   4 = Usually   5 = Always

In the future I am planning to _____

_____ develop more friends by being a better friend.

_____ display empathy to others by helping everyone possible.

_____ be a Triple A Person…I will "Be Ambitious And Accountable."

_____ display regular acts of kindness to as many people as possible.

_____ consider if my actions will "Help Or Hurt" me or others.

_____ "Be Smart; Don't Start" anything that might be a harmful habit.

_____ consider how my MOM would like me to "Walk Our Words."

_____ SMILE more often because it "Sure Makes It Lots Easier."

_____ remember that if somebody bullies me I'll "Walk Away Today!

_____ not be a BULLY because "Being Unfriendly Lessens Liking You."

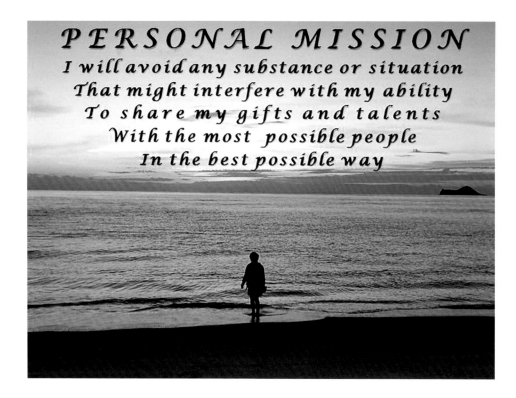

In conclusion…remember that you will always have more friends if you avoid being a BULLY because…Being Unfriendly Lessens Liking You. Develop close friends who will help you experience a happy life. You will have a better chance of experiencing a happy life if you are guided by this as your Personal Mission.

I will avoid any substance or situation
That might interfere with my ability
To share my gifts and talents
With the most possible people
In the best possible way!

Please write out the above Personal Mission.

_____

_____

_____

_____

_____

BULLY

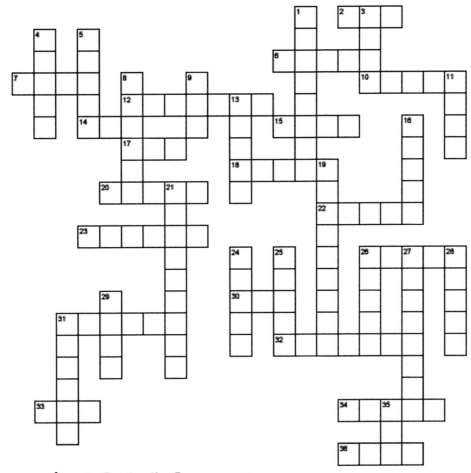

www.CharacterConstructionCompany.com

ACROSS

2 Always Seek Knowledge
6 Control All Negativism Develop Optimism
7 Be Ambitious And Accountable
10 Plan On Winning Everyone's Respect
12 Exercising My Personal Actions To Help You
14 Help Or Hurt
15 Compassion And Respect Everyday
17 Always Speak Kindly
18 People's Offensive Words Eliminate Respect
20 Love Education Achieve Respect Now
22 Success Often Requires Rescinding Yourself
23 Issuing Negative Statements Usually Leaves Turmoil
26 Success Takes A Realistic Try

30 Walk Our Words
31 Fabulous Relationships Inspire Empathy Not Drama
32 Recognizing Everyone's Strengths Produces Exceptional Caring Teams
33 To Respect Yourself
34 Perpetually Offering Wisdom Elevates Respect
36 Always Care To Share

DOWN

1 Great Relationships Always Discourage Unkind Attitudes; Treasure Education
3 Some Things Offend People
4 Debilitating Rumors Activate Malicious Attitudes
5 Try Engaging All Children Happily
8 Bullies Eliminate Happiness And Victimize Everyone

9 Meanness Always Destroys
11 Respect Others; Share Empathy
13 Habits And Purpose Please You
16 Being Unfriendly Lessens Liking You
19 Respect All People
21 Reflecting Our Leaders' Example Makes Our Deeds Endure Lifelong
24 Perpetually Offending Will Erode Respect
25 Pushing Over Welldoers Eliminates Respect
26 Sure Makes It Lots Easier
27 Always Trying To Improve Takes Unswerving Dedication Everyday
28 To Enjoy A Spirited Encounter
29 Never Insult Compliment Everyone
31 Forget Undoing The Undoable; Refocus Efforts
35 Walk Away Today

BULLY

Circle the hidden words in the grid. When you are done finding the words, circle the unused letters at the top of the grid that spell out a hidden message. Pick the words out from left to right, top line to bottom line. Words are formed horizontally, vertically and diagonally in all directions. As you circle the words attempt to recall the definition of their acronyms. Enjoy!

```
B  L  E  F  I  N  G  A  S  K  U  N  M  A  D  F
R  E  T  I  R  E  E  M  P  A  T  H  Y  S  P  N
D  D  L  C  Y  I  O  A  L  N  E  S  T  S  O  S
S  O  E  S  E  N  E  D  T  S  I  O  L  I  W  K
M  M  B  K  T  P  I  N  N  T  P  C  H  N  E  R
I  E  A  G  Y  A  S  O  D  A  I  U  E  O  R  A
L  L  A  R  Z  T  R  E  L  G  C  T  B  R  H  P
E  O  A  T  Q  C  N  T  R  A  Y  E  U  H  K  A
D  R  F  C  W  R  P  A  M  T  H  R  R  D  Z  S
T  F  M  W  A  O  D  A  A  A  Z  W  T  G  E  O
L  U  K  E  W  U  R  W  V  M  E  V  P  K  G  R
U  T  L  E  A  D  T  E  Y  Z  R  Y  P  P  A  H
S  U  R  T  S  Y  L  L  U  B  A  R  E  W  O  P
N  R  E  L  T  S  O  R  R  Y  C  S  K  Q  F  W
I  E  L  N  C  H  C  A  E  T  O  S  W  L  W  W
K  R  E  S  A  E  T  N  D  R  A  P  X  W  O  W
```

www.CharacterConstructionCompany.com

ACTS	DRAMA	MAD	SMILE
ASK	EMPATHY	NICE	SORRY
ASK	FRIEND	POWER	START
ATTITUDE	FUTURE	POWER	STOP
BAAA	GRADUATE	POWER	TEACH
BEHAVE	HAPPY	RESPECT	TEASE
BULLY	HOH	ROLE MODEL	TRY
CANDO	INSULT	ROSA PARKS	WAT
CARE	LEARN	ROSE	WOW

Designate the "Lesson of the Week" by listing an acronym or quote to share with everyone.

1. _____

2. _____

3. _____

4. _____

5. _____

6. _____

7. _____

8. _____

9. _____

10. _____

11. _____

12. _____

13. _____

14. _____

15. _____

16. _____

17. _____

18. _____

19. _____

20. _____

21. _____

22. _____

23. _____

24. _____

25. _____

26. _____

27. _____

28. _____

29. _____

30. _____

31. _____

32. _____

33. _____

34. _____

35. _____

36. _____

PERSONAL MISSION

"I will avoid_____

_____

_____

_____

_____."

CHAMPIONS*…if you pledge to help this person keep their promises please initial below!

CHAMPS Enter your CHAMPIONS' names, if they agree to help, ask them to initial and date.

Champions' Names	Champions' Signature	Course Start Date	Completion Date
1. _____	_____	__/__/__	__/__/__
2. _____	_____	__/__/__	__/__/__

CHAMPS list what you would like to promise by finishing the following statement of what you…will or will not do… (Use additional pages as needed)

In the future I PROMISE to myself, family and friends that I…

1. _____ __/__/__
2. _____ __/__/__
3. _____ __/__/__
4. _____ __/__/__
5. _____ __/__/__
6. _____ __/__/__
7. _____ __/__/__
8. _____ __/__/__
9. _____ __/__/__
10. _____ __/__/__
11. _____ __/__/__
12. _____ __/__/__
13. _____ __/__/__
14. _____ __/__/__
15. _____ __/__/__

*CHAMPIONS: Citizens Help Activate My Promises In Our Neighborhood

*PROMISE: People Respect Our Motivation If Sincerely Exercised

16. _____ ___/___/___

17. _____ ___/___/___

18. _____ ___/___/___

19. _____ ___/___/___

20. _____ ___/___/___

21. _____ ___/___/___

22. _____ ___/___/___

23. _____ ___/___/___

24. _____ ___/___/___

25. _____ ___/___/___

26. _____ ___/___/___

27. _____ ___/___/___

28. _____ ___/___/___

29. _____ ___/___/___

30. _____ ___/___/___

31. _____ ___/___/___

32. _____ ___/___/___

33. _____ ___/___/___

34. _____ ___/___/___

35. _____ ___/___/___

36. _____ ___/___/___

37. _____ ___/___/___

38. _____ ___/___/___

39. _____ ___/___/___

40. _____ ___/___/___

41. _____ ___/___/___

42. _____ ___/___/___

43. _____ ___/___/___

44. _____ ___/___/___

45. _____ ___/___/___

46. _____ ___/___/___

47. _____ ___/___/___

48. _____ ___/___/___

49. _____ ___/___/___

50. _____ ___/___/___

51. _____ ___/___/___

52. _____ ___/___/___

53. _____ ___/___/___

54. _____ ___/___/___

55. _____ ___/___/___

56. _____ ___/___/___

57. _____ ___/___/___

58. _____ ___/___/___

59. _____ ___/___/___

60. _____ ___/___/___

61. _____ ___/___/___

62. _____ ___/___/___

63. _____ ___/___/___

64. _____ ___/___/___

65. _____ ___/___/___

FRIEND CLUB
Recommendation Form

1.   CHAMP'S Name and Date…

     _____   ___/___/___

2.   The CHAMP has completed all of the course activities…

     _____ (Yes)   _____ (No)

3.   The CHAMP… (if applicable)

     _____ (did)   _____ (did not)   receive at least eighty percent on the final test.

4.   The CHAMP…

     Is fulfilling (circle one):   all   most   some   none   of their promises.

5.   We (CHAMPIONS Names)…

     (Print) _____   (Sign) _____

     (Print) _____   (Sign) _____

6.   Recommend that…

     (CHAMP'S name) _____ receive a

     FRIEND CLUB certificate and become an official member of the FRIEND CLUB!

Congratulations

_____

(CHAMP)

Has completed the BULLY Course and is an official member

of the

FRIEND CLUB

Fabulous Relationships Inspire Empathy Not Drama

Change Lives Undo Bullying

_____   _____

(CHAMPION/Date)   (CHAMPION/Date)

_____

(FRIEND CLUB)

GLOSSARY

TERM	PAGE	DESCRIPTION
ACTS	44	Always Care To Share
Apology Plan	26	"The five steps of an apology plan…"
Argument	46	"The only way to win an argument is not to argue."
ASK	33	Always Seek Knowledge
ASK	33	Always Speak Kindly
ATTITUDE	50	Always Trying To Improve Takes Unswerving Dedication Everyday
BAAA	17	Be Ambitious And Accountable
Be Smart	42, 43	Be Smart; Don't Start
BEHAVE	11	Bullies Eliminate Happiness And Victimize Everyone
Bullied?	29	"What should you do if you are bullied?"
BULLY	8	Being Unfriendly Lessens Liking You
CANDO	39	Control All Negativism; Develop Optimism
CARE	44	Compassion And Respect Everyday
CHAMPS	7	Connecting Hearts And Minds Propels Success
CHAMPIONS	7	Citizens Help Activate My Promises In Our Neighborhood
Children	12	"You can't teach children to behave better by making them…"
CLUB	7	Change Lives Undo Bullying
COACH	7	Channeling Our Actions Creates Happiness
DRAMA	14	Debilitating Rumors Activate Malicious Attitudes
EMPATHY	14	Exercising My Personal Actions To Help You
Find Friend	22	"If you want to find a friend, be a friend."
Five C's	34	"Connect, Challenge, Channel, Check, Confidence"
FRIEND	13	Fabulous Relationships Inspire Empathy Not Drama
FRIEND CLUB	64	FRIEND CLUB Recommendation Form
FRIEND Certificate	65	FRIEND CLUB Certificate (Please copy)
FUTURE	54, 55	Forget Undoing The Undoable; Refocus Efforts
Glossary	66, 67	You are on this page…Gotcha!
GRADUATE	53	Great Relationships Always Discourage Unkind Attitudes; Treasure Education
HAPPY	52	Habits And Purpose Please You
HOH	41	Help Or Hurt?
INSULT	31	Issuing Negative Statements Usually Leaves Turmoil
LEARN	53	Love Education; Achieve Respect Now
Lesson of week	59, 60	Designate the lesson of the week
MAD	35	Meanness Always Destroys
Mothers	20	"If you can't say anything nice about somebody, don't say anything at all!"
NICE	30	Never Insult Compliment Everyone

TERM	PAGE	DESCRIPTION
Personal Mission	56	"I will avoid any substance or situation that might interfere…"
Personal Value	51	"The true test of our value is how we value ourselves."
POWER	37	Perpetually Offending Will Erode Respect
POWER	37	Purposely Offending With Every Response
POWER	37	Pushing Over Welldoers Eliminates Respect
POWER	37	People's Offensive Words Eliminate Respect
POWER	37	People's Offensive Words Exemplify Rudeness
POWER	38	Plan On Winning Everyone's Respect
POWER	38	Proving Our Worth Establishes Respect
POWER	38	Personal Optimism Will Encourage Respect
POWER	38	Pleasing Others With Everlasting Recognition
POWER	38	Perpetually Offering Wisdom Elevates Respect
POWER	37	"What makes Superman a hero…"
Problem	36	"Is it the problem or how we react to the problem…"
Professor	68	The Professor, Skipper and Mary Ann
PROMISES	61-63	People Respect Our Motivation If Sincerely Exercised
Puzzle	57	BULLY Crossword
Puzzle	58	BULLY Word Find
RESPECT	15	Recognizing Everyone's Strengths Produces Exceptional Caring Teams
ROLE MODEL	39	Reflecting Our Leaders' Example Makes Our Deeds Endure Lifelong
Rosa Parks	32	Respect All People
ROSE	28	Respect Others; Share Empathy
SMILE	21	Sure Makes It Lots Easier
SORRY	25	Success Often Requires Rescinding Yourself
START	19	Success Takes A Realistic Try
STOP	27	Some Things Offend People
TEACH	34	Try Engaging All Children Happily
Teacher	24	"Let's discover your strengths and build on them; I am a teacher!"
TEASE	45	To Enjoy A Spirited Encounter
Three desires	23	"To belong, to be needed, to be loved…"
Three questions	40	"Is it necessary? Is it true? Is it kind?"
Thumbs Up	16	Give a "Thumbs Up" to our first responders
TRY	18, 19	To Respect Yourself
WAT	47	Walk Away Today
WOW	48, 49	Walk Our Words

The Professor, Skipper and Mary Ann

Mr. Brummond began developing his successful anti-bullying tools and techniques while serving as a music educator and school district administrator. Mrs. Brummond added her expertise with her knowledge of human interaction acquired during her career serving as a college administrator. For over a decade Skipper, the CEO – Canine Executive Officer supervised the Character Construction Company CREW – Compassionately Reaching Everyone Worldwide.

The couple has two adult sons and several grandchildren. Their hobbies have included skiing, running marathons, mountain biking, model truck racing, sports fishing, competitive bass fishing, tennis, archery, and world travel.

Character Construction Company has developed this course to carry on the mission of the Blue Light Coalition, from Tacoma, Washington, of honoring our 24/7 protectors by providing meaningful educational programs throughout the world.

We encourage you to experience our other online courses to continue developing your communication skills. Character Construction Company is simply on a mission to help make the world a happier place!

Character Construction Company Courses

1. Change
2. Honesty
3. Attitude
4. Respect

5. Achievement
6. Choices
7. Trust
8. Empowerment

9. Relationships
10. Inspire
11. Self-worth
12. Teamwork

13. Integrity
14. Communication
15. Success
16. Hooked

Courses available at **www.LearningCharacter.com**